EASY HITS GUITAR TAB EDITION

Alfred's

Easy guitar songs

ROCK and POP

50 HITS FROM ACROSS THE DECADES

Produced by
Alfred Music
P.O. Box 10003
Van Nuys, CA 91410-0003
alfred.com

Printed in USA.

ISBN-10: 1-4706-2755-8
ISBN-13: 978-1-4706-2755-3

Cover Photos
Gibson Hummingbird courtesy of Gibson Brands • Duesenberg Dragster DC courtesy of Duesenberg Guitars, USA

contents

TITLE	ARTIST	

artist index

STRUM PATTERNS

Below are a number of suggested patterns that may be used while strumming the chords for the songs in this book. Think of these as starting points from which you may embellish, mix up, or create your own patterns.

Note the markings above the staff that indicate the direction of the strums.

⊓ indicates a downstroke

V indicates an upstroke

FINGERPICKING PATTERNS

Here are some fingerpicking patterns that may be used to arpeggiate chords where indicated in this book.
As with the strum patterns, these are starting points from which you may embellish, mix up, or create your own patterns.

Note the fingerings:
p = thumb
i = index finger
m = middle finger
a = ring finger

⊓ indicates a downstroke   ⋁ indicates an upstroke

Fingerpicking Pattern #1:

Fingerpicking Pattern #2:

Fingerpicking Pattern #3:

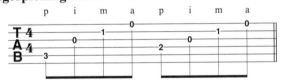

Fingerpicking Pattern #4:

Fingerpicking Pattern #5:

Fingerpicking Pattern #6:

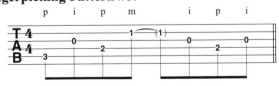

Fingerpicking Pattern #7:

Fingerpicking Pattern #8:

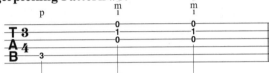

Fingerpicking Pattern #9:

Fingerpicking Pattern #10:

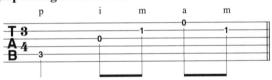

Fingerpicking Pattern #11:

Fingerpicking Pattern #12:

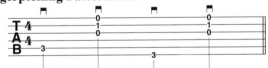

Fingerpicking Pattern #13:

Fingerpicking Pattern #14:

ALL ABOUT THAT BASS

Use Suggested Strum Pattern #3 for Verse and Chorus
Use Suggested Strum Pattern #6 for Pre-chorus

Words and Music by
MEGHAN TRAINOR and KEVIN KADISH

Moderately bright

Intro:

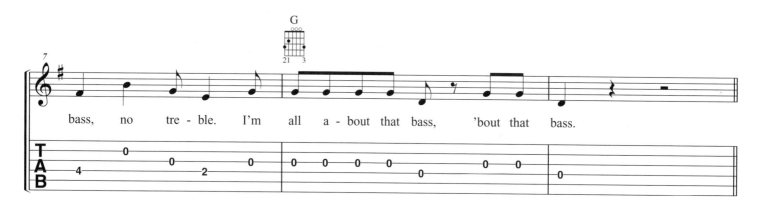

Verse:

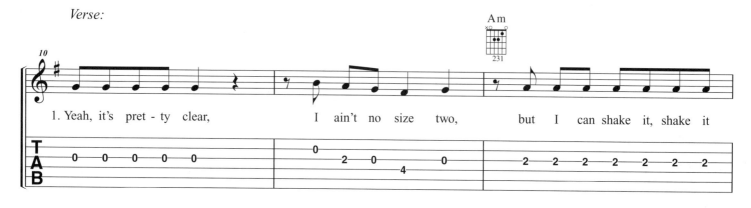

All About That Bass - 4 - 1

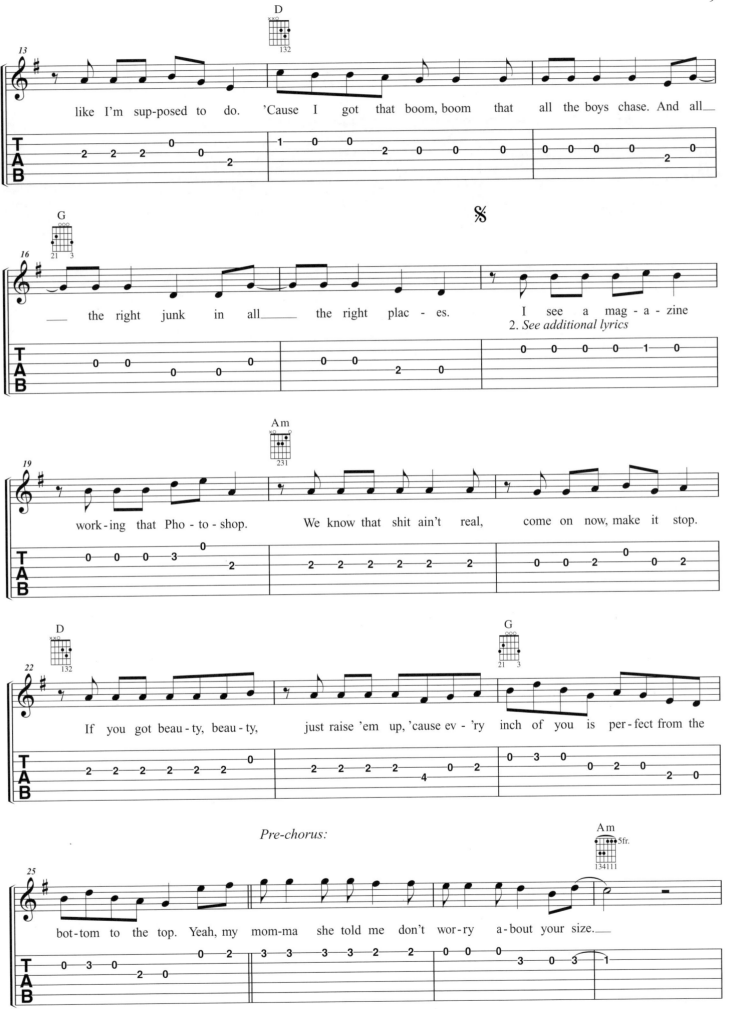

Verse 2:
I'm bringing booty back
Go ahead and tell them skinny bitches Hey
No, I'm just playing I know you think you're fat,
But I'm here to tell you that,
Every inch of you is perfect from the bottom to the top
(To Pre-chorus:)

ALL ALONG THE WATCHTOWER

Words and Music by
BOB DYLAN

Use Suggested Strum Pattern #1 (all downstrokes)

Moderately

All Along the Watchtower - 2 - 1

Verse 3:
All along the watchtower, princes kept the view.
While all the women came and went, barefoot servants, too.
Well, outside in the cold distance, a wildcat did growl.
Two riders were approaching and the wind began to howl.
(To Outro:)

BAD TO THE BONE

Words and Music by
GEORGE THOROGOOD

Suggested Strum Pattern: See Bars 2 and 3

Bad to the Bone - 3 - 1

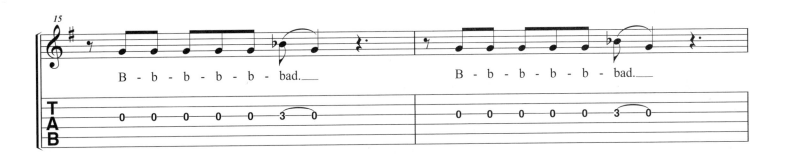

To Coda ⊕ | 1.

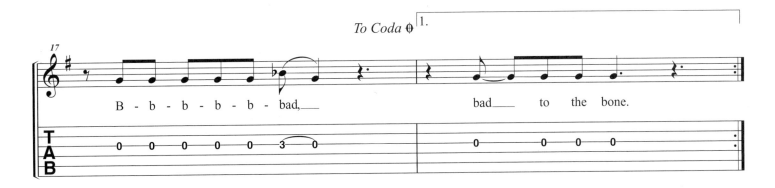

2.

Guitar Solo:

Bad to the Bone - 3 - 2

D.S. ℅ al Coda

⊕ *Coda*

bad___ to the bone.

N.C.

Verse 2:
I broke a thousand hearts
Before I met you.
I'll break a thousand more, baby,
Before I am through.
I wanna be yours, pretty baby,
Yours and yours alone.
I'm here to tell ya, honey,
That I'm bad to the bone,
Bad to the bone.
B-b-b-b-b-b-b bad,
B-b-b-b-b-b-b bad.
B-b-b-b-b-b-b bad,
Bad to the bone.
(To Guitar Solo:)

Verse 3:
Now, when I walk the streets,
Kings and Queens step aside.
Every woman I meet, heh, heh,
They all stay satisfied.
I wanna tell you, pretty baby,
What I see I make my own.
And I'm here to tell ya, honey,
That I'm bad to the bone,
Bad to the bone.
B-b-b-b-b-b-b bad,
B-b-b-b-b-b-b bad.
B-b-b-b-b-b-b bad,
Whoo, bad to the bone.
(To Coda)

COLOUR MY WORLD

Words and Music by
JAMES PANKOW

Use Suggested Strum Pattern #13

Slowly ♩. = 52

BEHIND BLUE EYES

**Use Suggested Strum Pattern #6
or Fingerpicking Pattern #6**

Moderately

Words and Music by
PETER TOWNSHEND

BIG YELLOW TAXI

Words and Music by
JONI MITCHELL

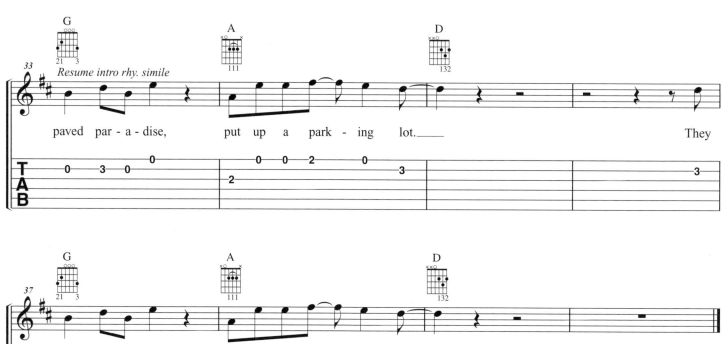

paved par-a-dise, put up a park-ing lot.____ They

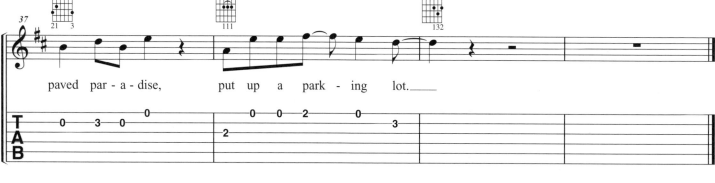

paved par-a-dise, put up a park-ing lot.____

Verse 2:
They took all the trees
Put 'em in a tree museum
And they charged the people
A dollar and a half just to see 'em
(To Chorus:)

Verse 3:
Hey, farmer, farmer
Put away that D.D.T. now
Give me spots on my apples
But leave me the birds and the bees. Please
(To Chorus:)

Verse 4:
Late last night
I heard the screen door slam
And a big yellow taxi
Took away my old man
(To Chorus:)

BOTH SIDES NOW
(Judy Collins Version)

**Use Suggested Strum Pattern #3
or Fingerpicking Pattern from Intro**

Words and Music by
JONI MITCHELL

Moderately

1. Rows and flows of an-gel hair___ and ice-cream cas-tles in the air,___
2.3. *See additional lyrics*

and feath-er can-yons ev-'ry-where. I've looked at clouds that way. But

now they on-ly block the sun,___ they rain and snow on ev-'ry-one.___

Both Sides Now - 3 - 1

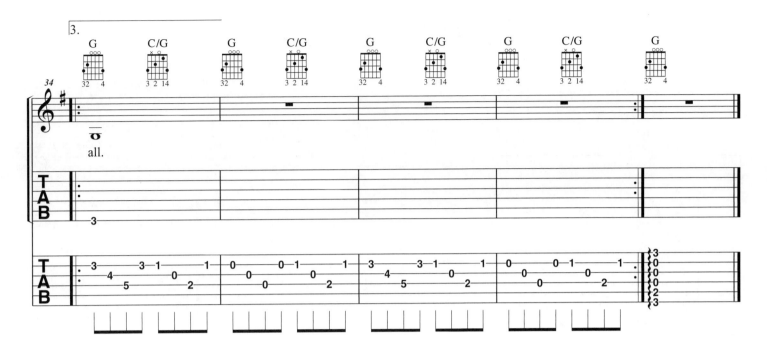

Verse 2:
Moons and Junes and Ferris wheels
The dizzy dancing way you feel
When every fairy tale comes real
I've looked at love that way
But now it's just another show
You leave 'em laughing when you go
And if you care, don't let them know
Don't give yourself away

Chorus 2:
I've looked at love from both sides, now
From win and lose, and still somehow
It's love's illusions I recall
I really don't know love at all

Verse 3:
Tears and fears and feeling proud
To say "I love you" right out loud
Dreams and schemes and circus crowds
I've looked at life that way
But now old friends are acting strange
They shake their heads, they say I've changed
Well, something's lost but something's gained
In living every day

Chorus 3:
I've looked at life from both sides, now
From win and lose, and still somehow
It's life's illusions I recall
I really don't know life at all

BROWN SUGAR

Use Suggested Strum Pattern #2

Words and Music by
MICK JAGGER and KEITH RICHARDS

Brown Sugar - 4 - 1

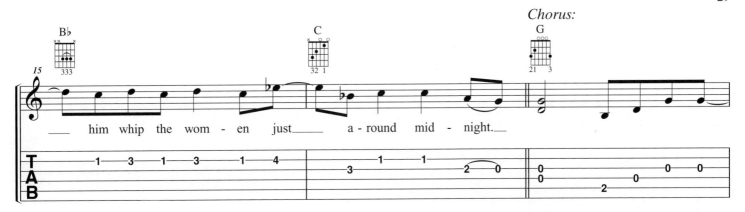

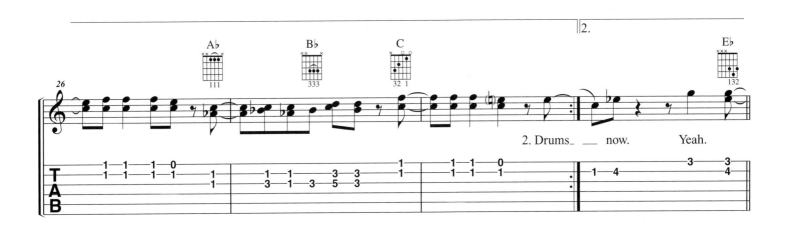

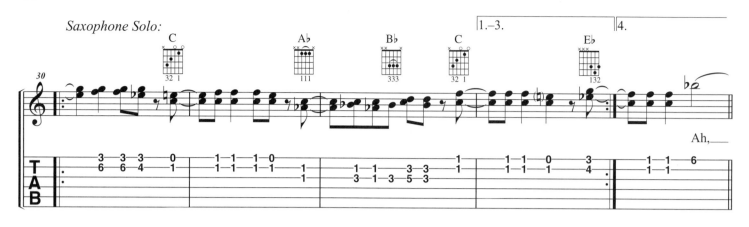

Saxophone Solo:

Ah,___

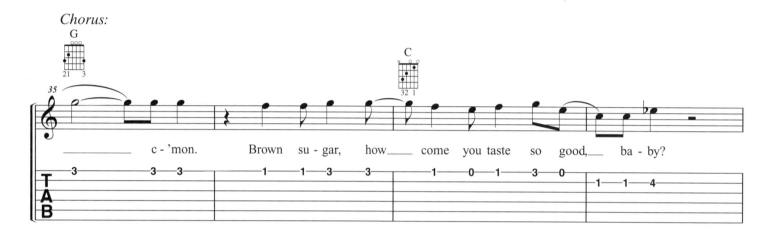

Chorus:

_____ c - 'mon.   Brown su - gar,   how___ come you taste   so good,___ ba - by?

D.S. 𝄋 al Coda

Brown su - gar,   just like a black girl   should,___ yeah.   3. Now,

⊕ Coda

just like a young girl   should,___ yeah,   yeah.___

Brown Sugar - 4 - 3

Verse 2:
Drums beating, cold English blood runs hot,
Lady of the house wondrin' where it's gonna stop.
House boy knows that he's doin' alright,
You should a heard him just around midnight.
(To Chorus:)

Verse 3:
I bet your mama was a tent show queen,
And all her boyfriends were sweet sixteen.
I'm no schoolboy but I know what I like,
You should have heard me just around midnight.
(To Chorus:)

Brown Sugar - 4 - 4

A CHANGE IS GONNA COME

Use Suggested Strum Pattern #13
or Fingerpicking Pattern #14

Words and Music by
SAM COOKE

Slowly

A Change Is Gonna Come - 2 - 1

Verse 2:
It's been too hard living but I'm afraid to die
'Cause I don't know what's up there beyond the sky.
It's been a long, a long time comin',
But I know, oh-oo-oh,
A change gon' come, oh, yes, it will.

Verse 3:
I go to the movie and I go downtown.
Somebody keep tellin' me don't hang around.
It's been a long, a long time comin',
But I know, oh-oo-oh,
A change gon' come, oh, yes, it will.
(To Bridge:)

Verse 4:
There've been times that I thought I couldn't last for long
But now I think I'm able to carry on.
It's been a long, a long time comin',
But I know, oh-oo-oh,
A change gon' come, oh, yes, it will.

CHANGES IN LATITUDES, CHANGES IN ATTITUDES

Words and Music by
JIMMY BUFFETT

Use Suggested Strum Pattern #1

Moderately

1. I took off___ for a week - end last month just to try and re - call___ the whole year.
2.3. *See additional lyrics*

All of the fac - es and all___ of the plac - es,___ won - d'rin' where they all dis - ap - peared.

I did-n't pon - der the ques - tion too long; I was hun-gry and went out for a___ bite. Ran

Changes in Latitudes, Changes in Attitudes - 3 - 1

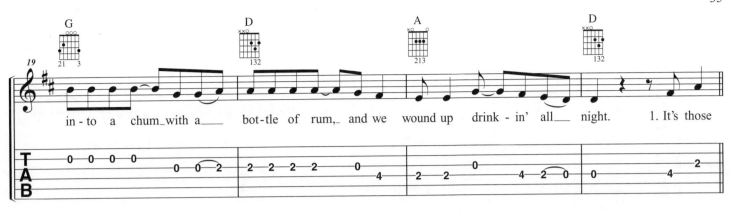

in-to a chum_with a___ bot-tle of rum,_ and we wound up drink-in' all___ night. 1. It's those

Chorus:

chang-es in lat - i-tudes, chang-es in at - ti-tudes; noth-ing re-mains_quite the same. With
2.3. *See additional lyrics*

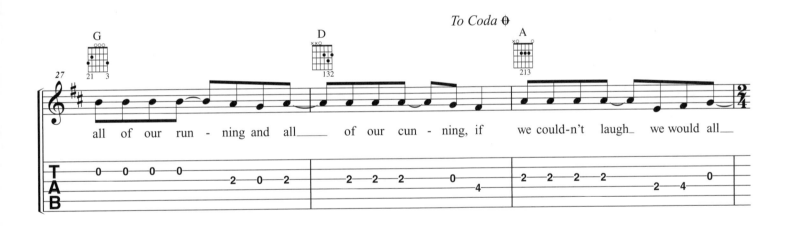

all of our run - ning and all___ of our cun - ning, if we could-n't laugh_ we would all___

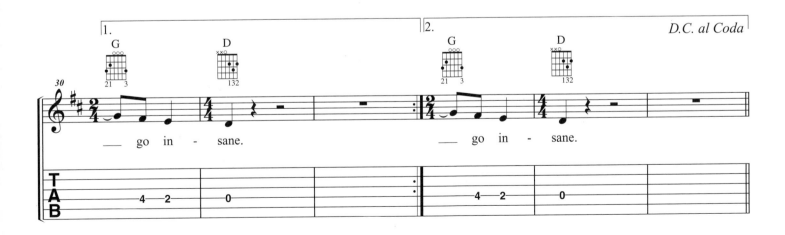

___ go in - sane. ___ go in - sane.

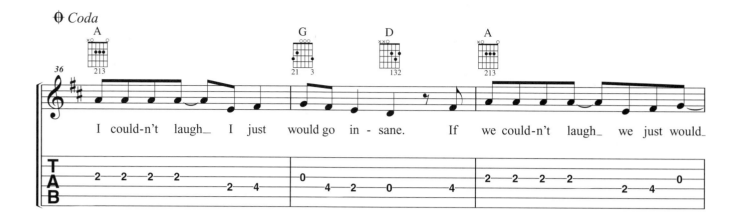

𝄌 *Coda*

I could-n't laugh_ I just would go in - sane. If we could-n't laugh_ we just would_

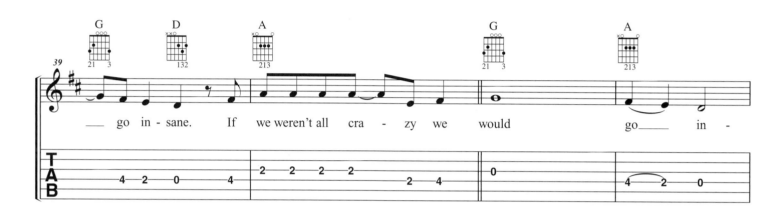

_ go in - sane. If we weren't all cra - zy we would go_____ in -

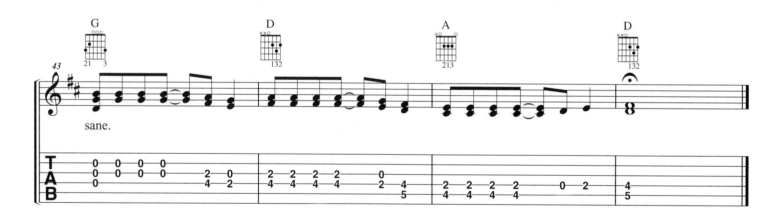

sane.

Verse 2:
Reading departure signs in some big airport
Reminds me of the places I've been.
Visions of good times that brought so much pleasure
Makes me want to go back again.
If it suddenly ended tomorrow,
I could somehow adjust to the fall.
Good times and riches and son of a bitches,
I've seen more than I can recall.

Chorus 2:
These changes in latitudes,
Changes in attitudes;
Nothing remains quite the same.
Through all of the islands and all of the highlands,
If we couldn't laugh we would all go insane.

Verse 3:
I think about Paris when I'm high on red wine;
I wish I could jump on a plane.
And so many nights I just dream of the ocean.
God, I wish I was sailin' again.
Oh, yesterdays are over my shoulder,
So I can't look back for too long.
There's just too much to see waiting in front of me,
And I know that I just can't go wrong.

Chorus 3:
With these changes in latitudes,
Changes in attitudes;
Nothing remains quite the same.
With all of my running and all of my cunning,
If I couldn't laugh I would all go insane.
(To Coda)

DANCING QUEEN

Words and Music by
**BENNY ANDERSSON, STIG ANDERSON
and BJORN ULVAEUS**

Use Suggested Strum Pattern #6

Dancing Queen - 3 - 1

CLASSICAL GAS

Use Suggested Strum Pattern #4 (begin at bar 8)

By MASON WILLIAMS

Freely

Moderately

44

COOL KIDS

Words and Music by
GRAHAM SIEROTA, JAMIE SIEROTA,
NOAH SIEROTA, SYDNEY SIEROTA,
JEFFERY DAVID SIEROTA and
JESIAH DZWONEK

Use Suggested Strum Pattern #1 (all downstrokes)

Cool Kids - 4 - 1

Verse 2:
He sees them talking with a big smile, but they haven't got a clue.
Yeah, they're living the good life; can't see what he is going through.
They're driving fast cars but they don't know where they're going;
In the fast lane, living without knowing.
And he says,
(To Chorus:)

DO YOU WANT TO KNOW A SECRET

Use Suggested Strum Pattern #4
or Fingerpicking Pattern #4

Words and Music by
JOHN LENNON and PAUL McCARTNEY

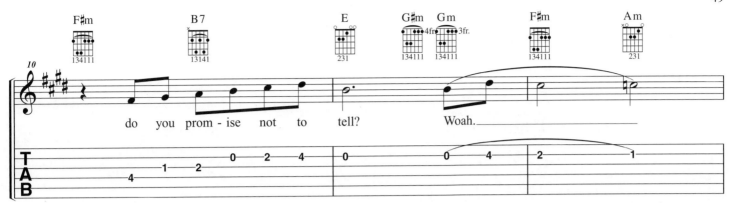

do you prom-ise not to tell? Woah._____

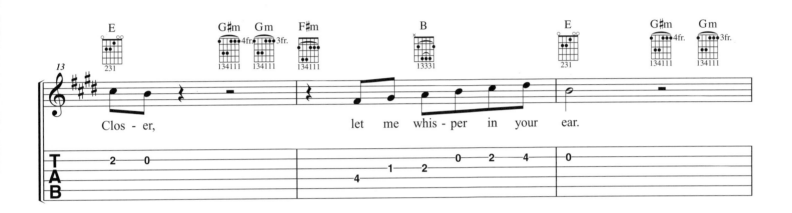

Clos - er, let me whis - per in your ear.

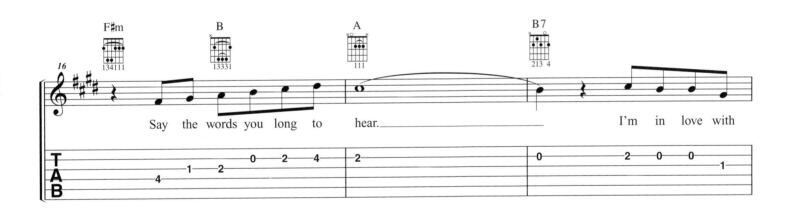

Say the words you long to hear._____ I'm in love with

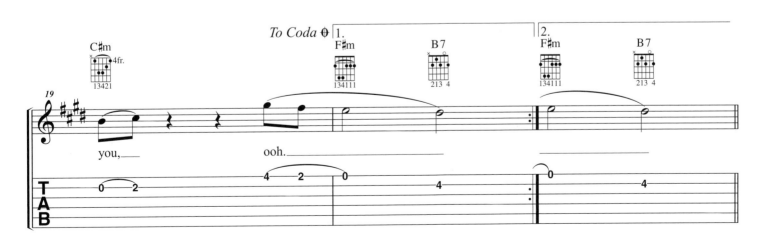

you,___ ooh._____

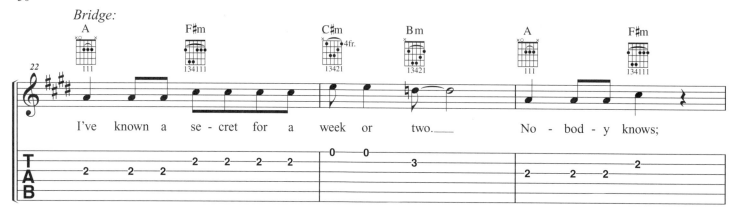

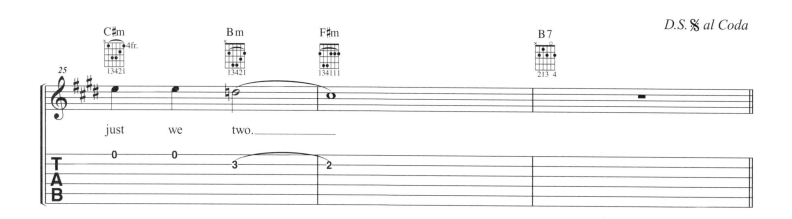

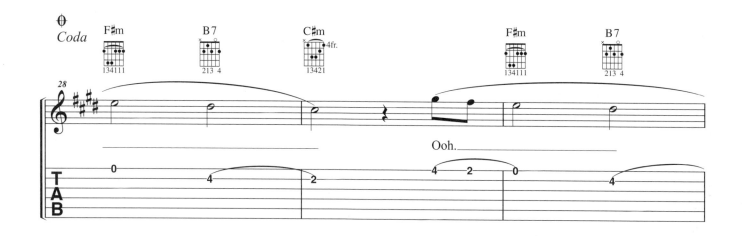

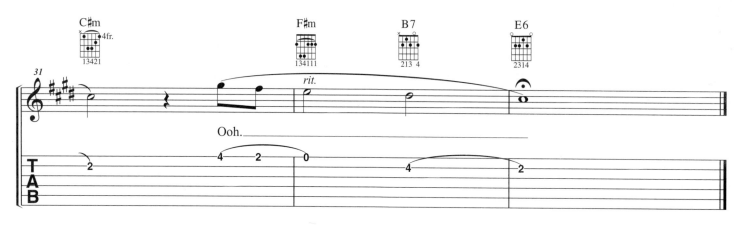

DON'T STOP BELIEVIN'

Words and Music by
JONATHAN CAIN, NEAL SCHON
and STEVE PERRY

Use Suggested Strum Pattern #2

Don't Stop Believin' - 5 - 1

Verse 3:

Work-in' hard_ to get my fill,_ ev-'ry-bod - y wants a thrill.____

Pay-in' an - y -thing to roll the dice_ just one more_ time.____

Some will win,__ some will lose,_ some are born_ to sing the blues.__

D.S. % al Coda

Oh, the mov - ie nev - er ends,_ it goes on and on__ and on___ and on._

EVERYTHING IS AWESOME
(Awesome Remixxx!!!)
(from The Lego Movie)

Lyrics by
SHAWN PATTERSON, ANDY SAMBERG,
AKIVA SCHAFFER, JORMA TACCONE,
JOSHUA BARTHOLOMEW and LISA HARRITON

Music by
SHAWN PATTERSON

Use Suggested Strum Pattern #1
Moderately fast

Everything Is Awesome (Awesome Remixxx!!!) - 5 - 1

Everything Is Awesome (Awesome Remixxx!!!) - 5 - 2

58

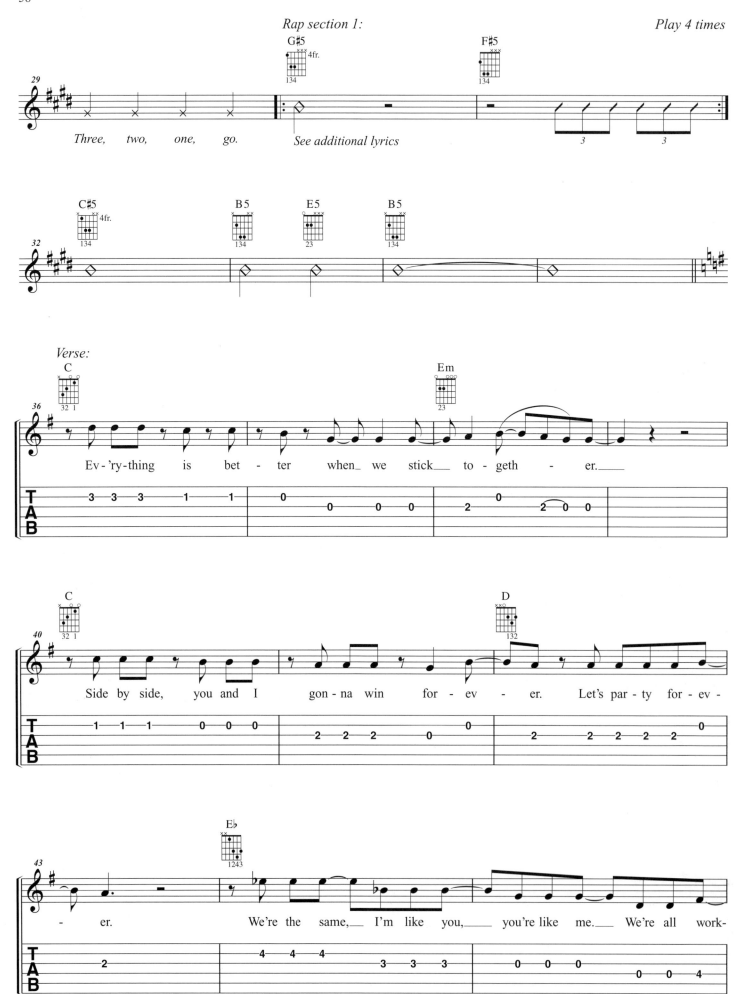

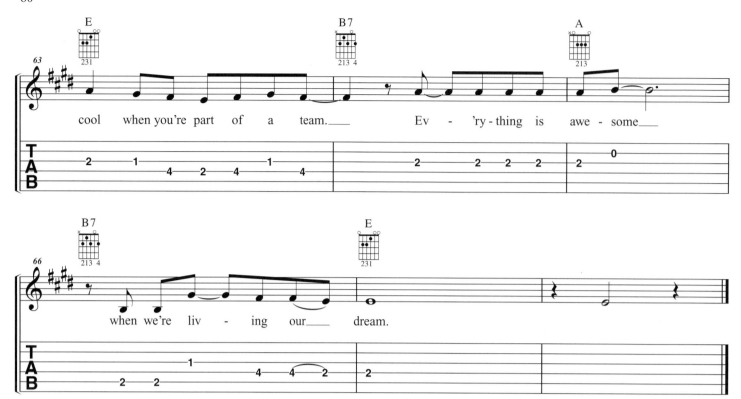

cool   when you're part of a team.___   Ev - 'ry - thing is   awe - some___

when we're   liv - ing   our___   dream.

Rap section 1:
Have you heard the news, everyone's talking
Life is good 'cause everything's awesome
Lost my job, it's a new opportunity
More free time for my awesome community.

I feel more awesome than an awesome possum
Dip my body in chocolate frostin'
Three years later, wash off the frostin'
Smellin' like a blossom, everything is awesome
Stepped in mud, got new brown shoes
It's awesome to win, and it's awesome to lose (it's awesome to lose).

Rap section 2:
Blue skies, bouncy springs
We just named two awesome things
A Nobel prize, a piece of string
You know what's awesome? EVERYTHING!

Dogs with fleas, allergies,
A book of Greek antiquities
Brand new pants, a very old vest
Awesome items are the best.

Trees, frogs, clogs
They're awesome
Rocks, clocks, and socks
They're awesome
Figs, and jigs, and twigs
That's awesome
Everything you see, or think, or say
Is awesome.

FERNANDO

Use Suggested Strum Pattern #3

Words and Music by
BENNY ANDERSSON, STIG ANDERSON
and BJORN ULVAEUS

Moderately

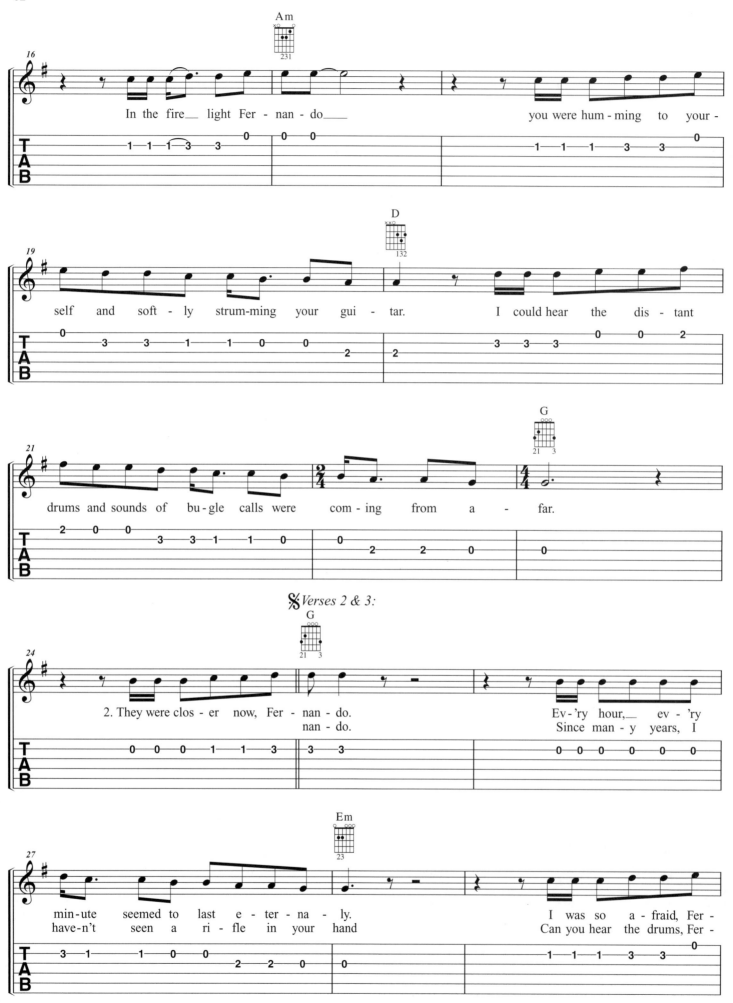

FORGET YOU

Words and Music by
CHRISTOPHER BROWN, PHILIP LAWRENCE, ARI LEVINE,
BRUNO MARS and THOMAS CALLAWAY

Use Suggested Strum Pattern #6

Moderately bright

Forget You - 4 - 1

To Coda
1.
2.
Bridge:
F C C Em
for - get you. 2. Now, Now, ba - by, ba - by, ba - by, why you
Am Dm G7 Em E7
wan - na, wan - na hurt me so bad? I tried to tell my ma - ma, but she
Am G/B C A7 D7 G7
D.S. al Coda
told me, "This is one for your dad." See you
Coda
C
Uh.

GHOSTBUSTERS

Words and Music by
RAY PARKER, JR.

Use Suggested Strum Pattern #4

Moderately

Intro:

Play 3 times

Ghost - bust - ers!

1. If there's

Verses 1 & 2:

some - thing   strange
see - ing   things

in   your   neigh - bor - hood.
run - ning through your   head.

Ghostbusters - 6 - 1

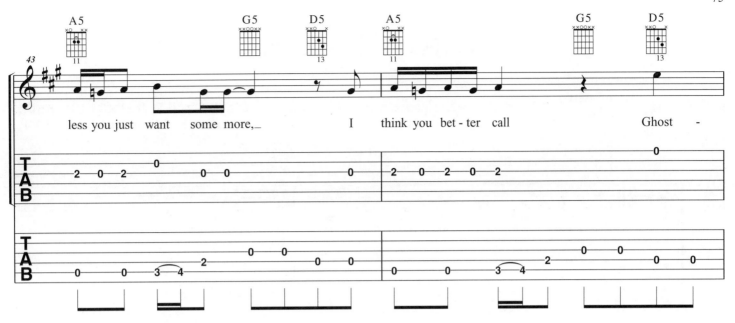

less you just want some more,__ I think you bet - ter call Ghost -

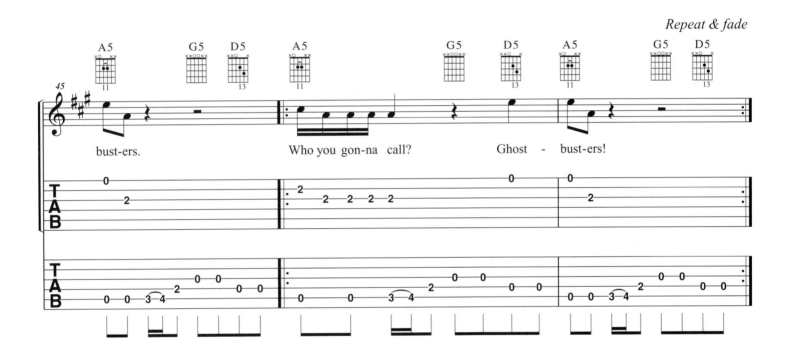

Repeat & fade

bust-ers. Who you gon-na call? Ghost - bust-ers!

Verse 3:
Who you gonna call?
Ghostbusters!
If you've had a dose of a freaky ghost,
Baby, you'd better call…
Ghostbusters!
Let me tell you something,
Bustin' makes me feel good.
I ain't afraid of no ghost.
I ain't afraid of no ghost.
(To Coda)

GIRL ON FIRE

Use Suggested Strum Pattern #5

Moderately

Words and Music by
BILLY SQUIER, JEFFREY BHAKSER,
ALICIA KEYS and SALAAM REMI

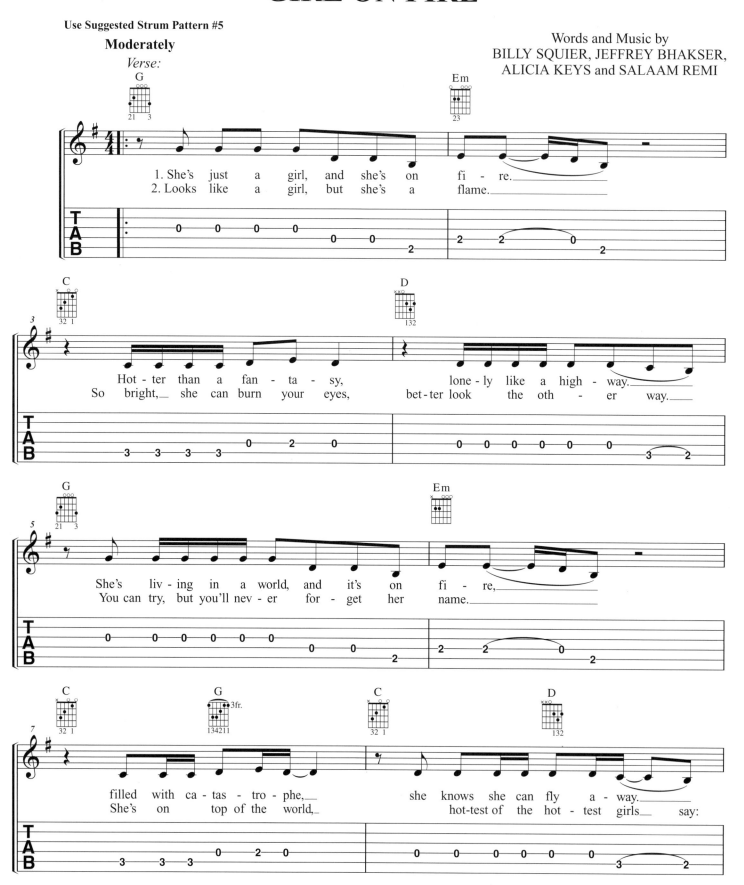

Girl on Fire - 4 - 1

Girl on Fire - 4 - 4

GRENADE
(acoustic live version)

Use Suggested Strum Pattern #6
or Fingerpick as shown in the Intro

Moderately

Words and Music by
CLAUDE KELLY, BRODY BROWN, PHILIP LAWRENCE,
ARI LEVINE, ANDREW WYATT and BRUNO MARS

1. Eas - y come, eas - y go, that's just how you live. Oh, take, take, take it all,
2. *See additional lyrics*

but you nev - er give. Should-'ve known you was trou - ble from the first kiss, had your

Grenade - 5 - 1

Verse 2:
Black, black, black and blue, beat me 'til I'm numb.
Tell the devil I said, "Hey" when you get back to where you're from.
Mad woman, bad woman, that's just what you are.
Yeah, you'll smile in my face then rip the brakes out my car.
(To Chorus:)

I DON'T WANT TO MISS A THING

Use Suggested Strum Pattern #1

(from *Armageddon*)

Words and Music by
DIANE WARREN

I Don't Want to Miss a Thing - 3 - 1

I CAN SEE CLEARLY NOW

Use Suggested Strum Pattern #7

Moderate reggae

Words and Music by
JOHNNY NASH

I Can See Clearly Now - 2 - 1

I SAW HER STANDING THERE

Use Suggested Strum Pattern #1
Moderately fast

Words and Music by
JOHN LENNON and PAUL McCARTNEY

I Saw Her Standing There - 3 - 1

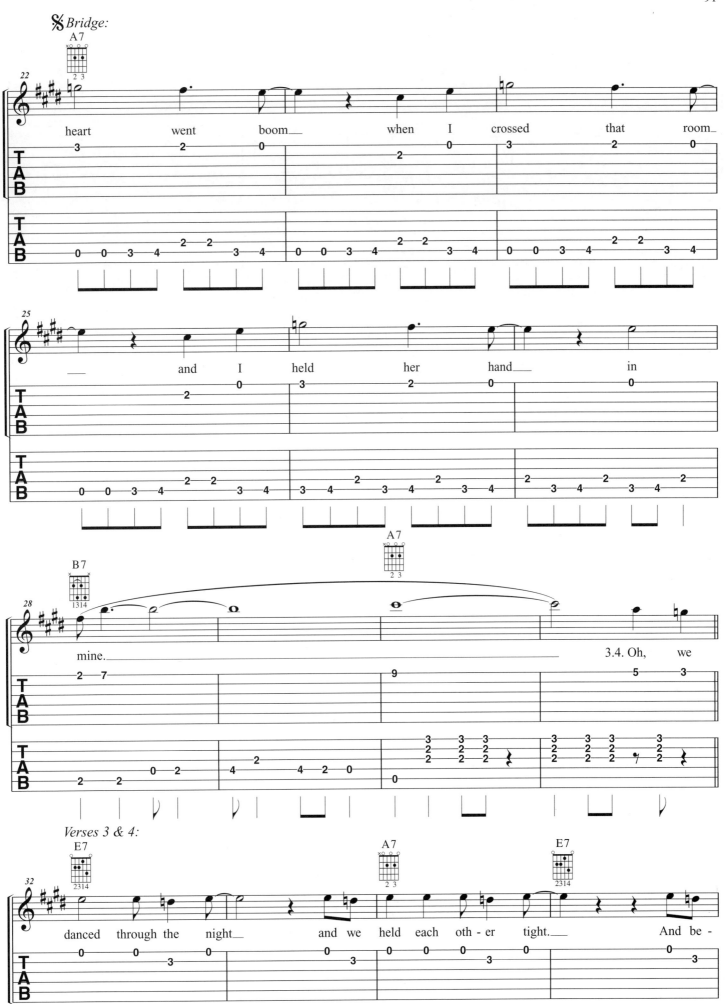

JAMES BOND THEME

By MONTY NORMAN

Use Suggested Strum Pattern #1 (all downstrokes)

Moderately fast

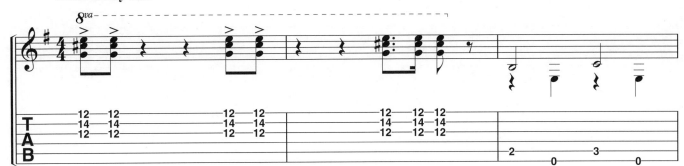

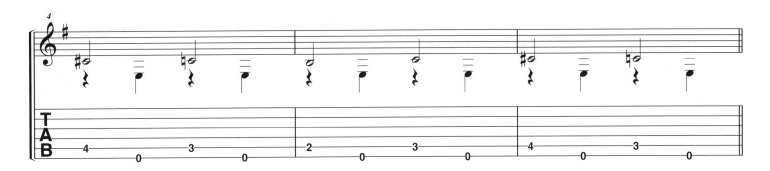

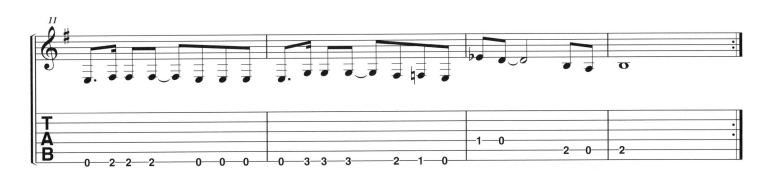

Jmaes Bond Theme - 3 - 1

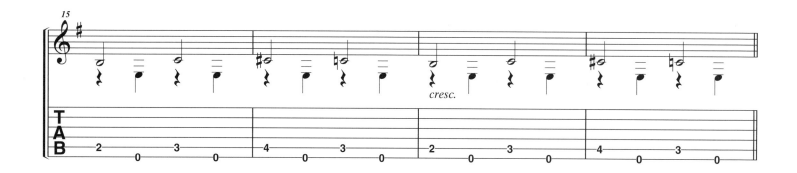

Swing feel

Moderately fast

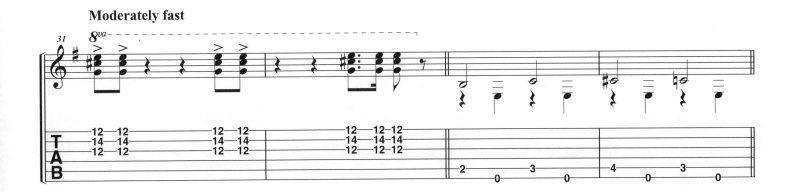

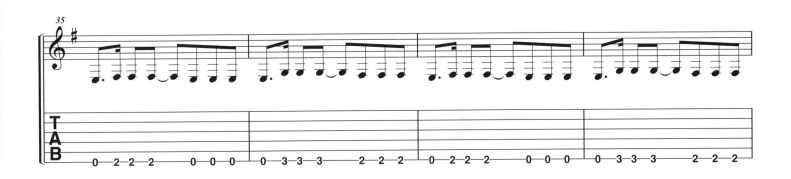

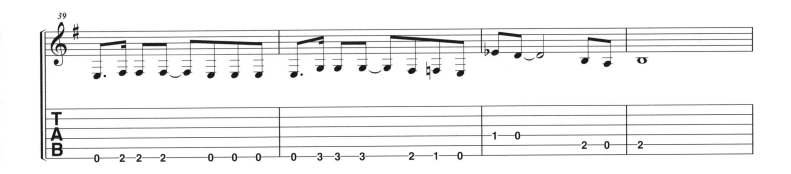

N.C.

Em(maj9)

Jmaes Bond Theme - 3 - 3

I SEE FIRE

Use Suggested Strum Pattern #6
or Fingerpicking Pattern #6

Words and Music by
ED SHEERAN

I See Fire - 6 - 1

I See Fire - 6 - 4

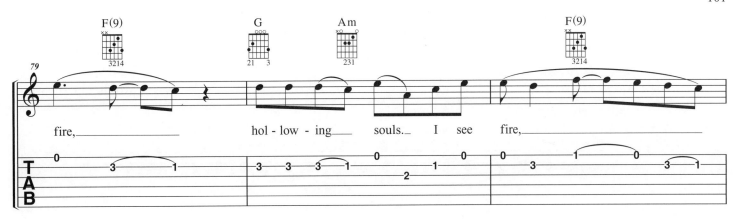

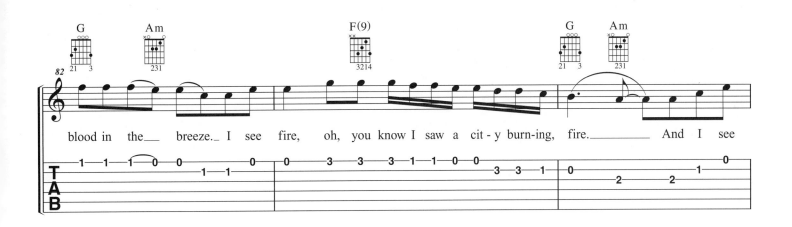

IF YOU LEAVE ME NOW

Use Suggested Strum Pattern #6
or Fingerpicking Pattern #6

Words and Music by
PETER CETERA

Moderately slow

If You Leave Me Now - 4 - 1

If You Leave Me Now - 4 - 2

JUMPIN' JACK FLASH

Words and Music by
MICK JAGGER and KEITH RICHARDS

Use Suggested Strum Pattern #6

Jumpin' Jack Flash - 5 - 1

Verse 3:
I was drowned, I was washed up and left for dead.
I fell down to my feet and I saw they bled.
I frowned at the crumbs of a crust of bread.
I was crowned with a spike right thru my head.
(To Chorus:)

JUST THE WAY YOU ARE (AMAZING)

Words and Music by
KHALIL WALTON, PETER HERNANDEZ,
PHILIP LAWRENCE, ARI LEVINE
and KHARI CAIN

Use Suggested Strum Pattern #2

Moderately

Just the Way You Are (Amazing) - 5 - 1

114

Just the Way You Are (Amazing) - 5 - 4

LAY LADY LAY

Use Suggested Strum Pattern #1

Moderately slow

Words and Music by
BOB DYLAN

1. Lay, la - dy, lay,___ lay a - cross my big brass bed.___
2.3. *See additional lyrics*

Lay, la - dy, lay,___ lay a - cross my big brass bed.___

What ev - er col - ors you have___

Lay Lady Lay - 3 - 1

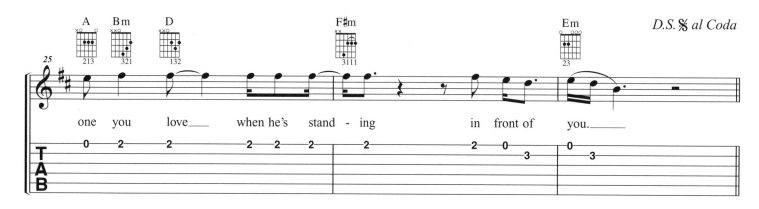

D.S. ⅔ al Coda

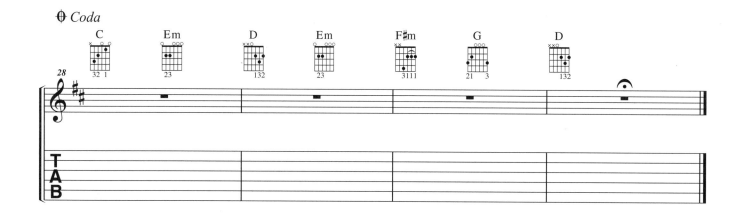

Verse 2:
Stay, lady, stay, stay with your man awhile.
Until the break of day, let me see you make him smile.
His clothes are dirty but his hands are clean.
And you're the best thing that he's ever seen.
Stay, lady, stay, stay with your man awhile.
(To Chorus:)

Verse 3:
Lay lady, lay lay across my big brass bed.
Stay, lady, stay, stay while the night is still ahead.
I long to see you in the morning light.
I long to reach for you in the night.
Stay, lady, stay, stay while the night is still ahead.
(To Chorus:)

LEAVING ON A JET PLANE

Use Suggested Strum Pattern #2

Words and Music by
JOHN DENVER

Moderately

Leaving on a Jet Plane - 3 - 1

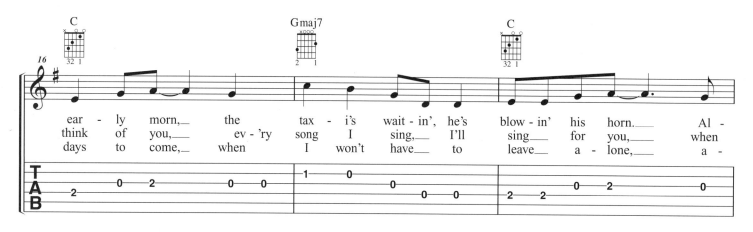

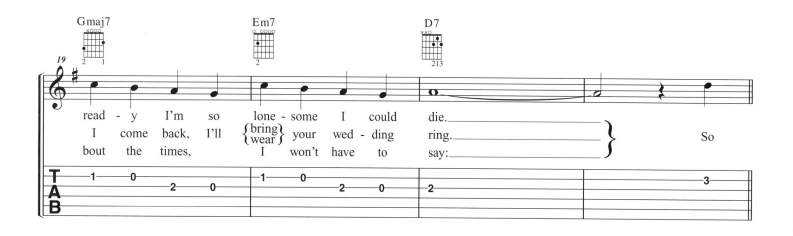

Chorus:

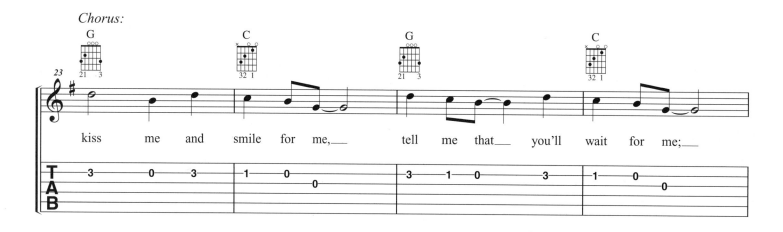

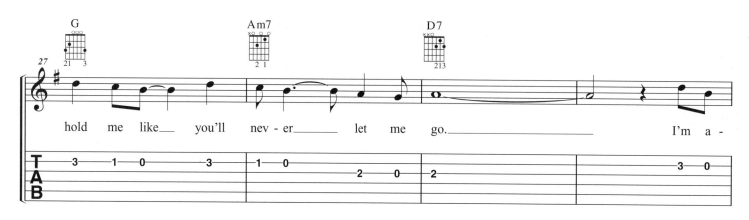

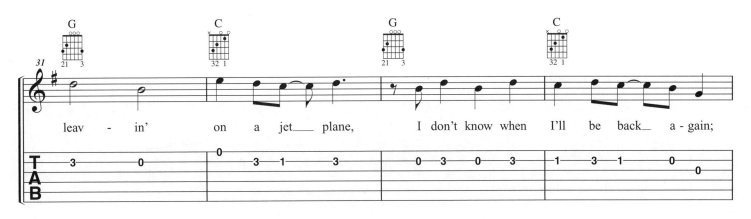

leav - in' on a jet___ plane, I don't know when I'll be back___ a-gain;

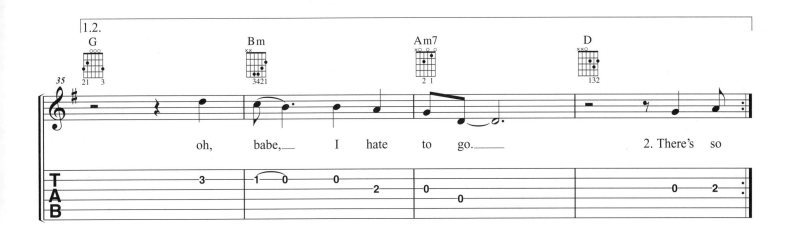

oh, babe,___ I hate to go.___ 2. There's so

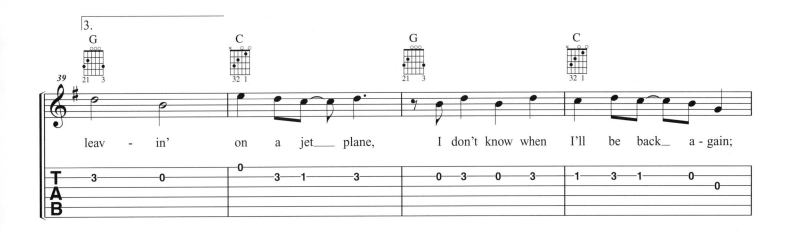

leav - in' on a jet___ plane, I don't know when I'll be back___ a-gain;

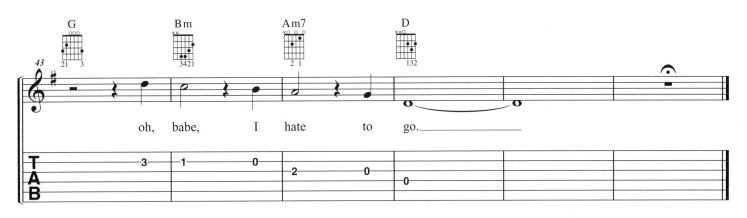

oh, babe, I hate to go._____

Leaving on a Jet Plane - 3 - 3

LET IT GO
(from Walt Disney's *Frozen*)

Use Suggested Strum Pattern #6

Music and Lyrics by
KRISTEN ANDERSON-LOPEZ
and ROBERT LOPEZ

Moderately, with a half-time feel

Verse 1:

Let It Go - 5 - 1

OVER THE RAINBOW

(As performed by Israel "Iz" Kamakawiwoʻole)

Music by
HAROLD ARLEN
Lyrics by
E.Y. HARBURG

Use Suggested Strum Pattern #7
Moderate reggae feel

Over the Rainbow - 3 - 1

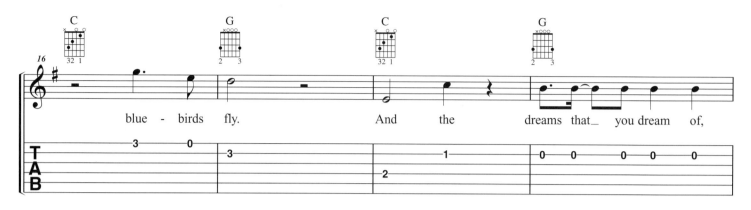

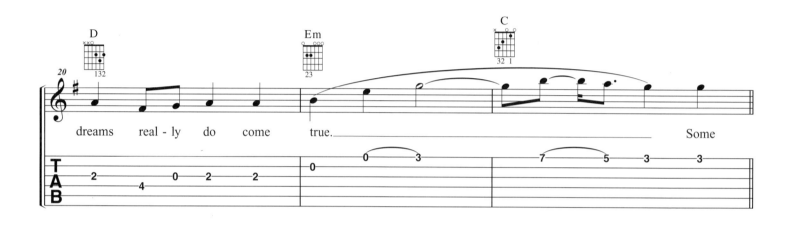

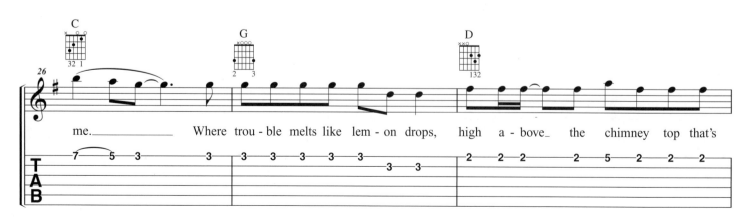

MARGARITAVILLE

Use Suggested Strum Pattern #2

Words and Music by
JIMMY BUFFETT

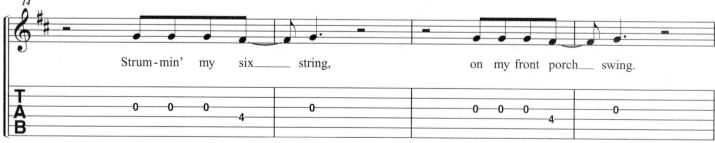

Margaritaville - 4 - 2

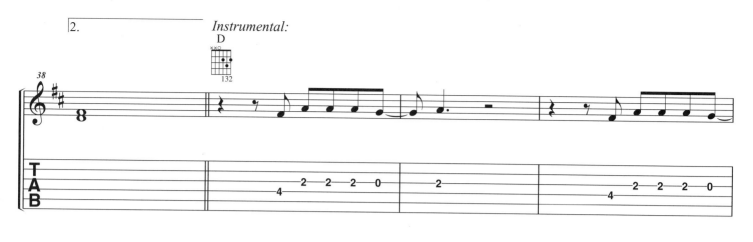

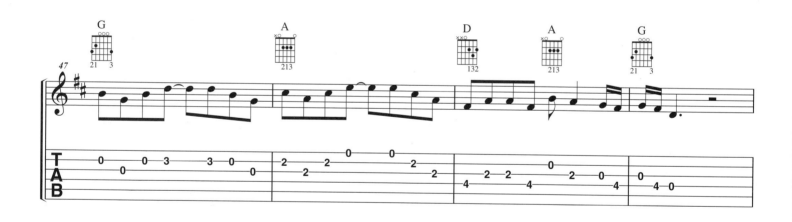

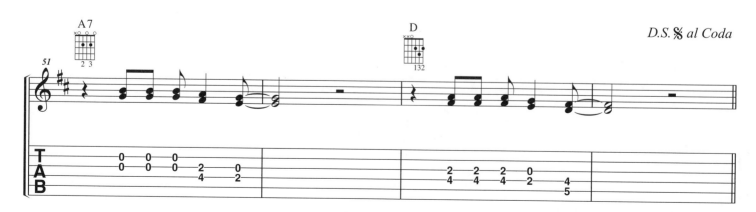

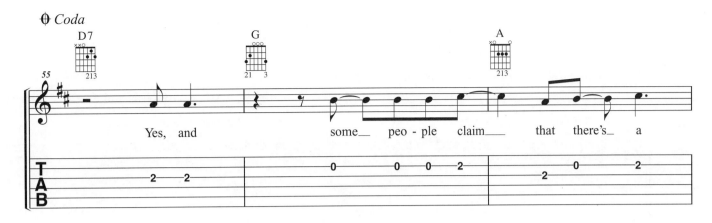

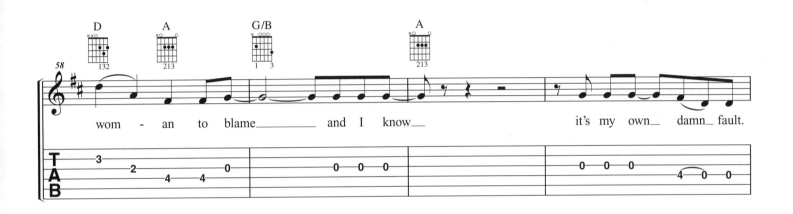

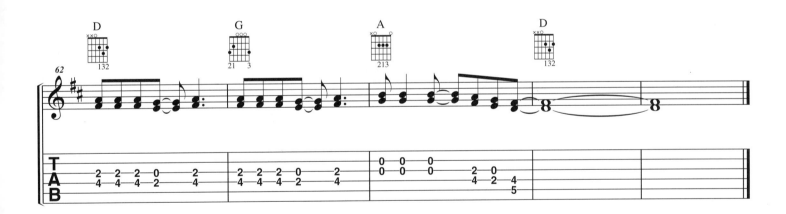

Verse 2:
Don't know the reason,
I stayed here all season
With nothing to show but this brand-new tattoo.
But it's a real beauty,
A Mexican cutie,
How it got here I haven't a clue.
(To Chorus:)

Verse 3
I blew out my flip-flop,
Stepped on a pop-top;
Cut my heel, had to cruise on back home.
But there's booze in the blender,
And soon it will render
That frozen concoction that helps me hang on.
(To Chorus:)

PAINT IT, BLACK

Use Suggested Strum Pattern #1 (all downstrokes)

Words and Music by
MICK JAGGER and KEITH RICHARDS

Verse 3:
I look inside myself and see my heart is black.
I see my red door, I must have it painted black.

Bridge 3:
Maybe then I'll fade away and not have to face the facts.
It's not easy facing up when your whole world is black.

Verse 4:
No more will my green sea go turn a deeper blue.
I could not foresee this thing happening to you.

Bridge 4:
If I look hard enough into the setting sun,
My love will laugh with me before the mornin' comes.
(To Verse 5:)

ROCKY MOUNTAIN HIGH

**Use Suggested Strum Pattern #6
or Fingerpicking Pattern #6**

Words and Music by
JOHN DENVER and MIKE TAYLOR

Rocky Mountain High - 3 - 1

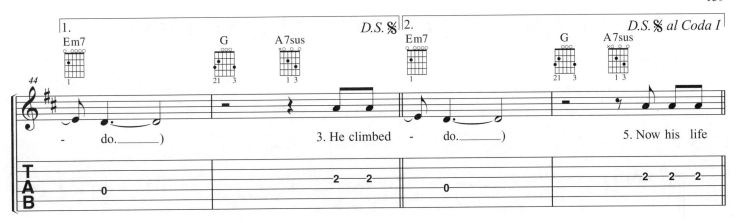

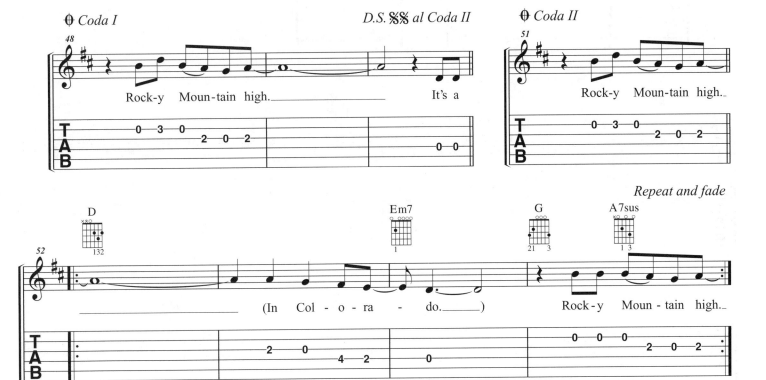

Verse 2:
When he first came to the mountains his life was far away,
On the road and hangin' by a song.
But the string's already broken and he doesn't really care.
It keeps changin' fast, and it don't last for long.
(To Chorus 1:)

Verse 3:
He climbed cathedral mountains, he saw silver clouds below.
He saw everything as far as you can see.
And they say that he got crazy once and he tried to touch the sun,
And he lost a friend but kept his memory.

Verse 4:
Now he walks in quiet solitude the forests and the streams,
Seeking grace in every step he takes.
His sight has turned inside himself to try and understand
The serenity of a clear blue mountain lake.

Chorus 2:
And the Colorado Rocky Mountain high,
I've seen it rainin' fire in the sky.
You can talk to God and listen to the casual reply.
Rocky Mountain high. (In Colorado.)
Rocky Mountain high. (In Colorado.)

Verse 5:
Now his life is full of wonder but his heart still knows some fear
Of a simple thing he cannot comprehend.
Why they try to tear the mountains down to bring in a couple more,
More people, more scars upon the land.

Chorus 3:
And the Colorado Rocky Mountain high,
I've seen it rainin' fire in the sky.
I know he'd be a poorer man if he never saw an eagle fly.
Rocky Mountain high.

Chorus 4:
It's a Colorado Rocky Mountain high.
I've seen it rainin' fire in the sky.
Friends around the campfire and everybody's high.
Rocky Mountain high. (In Colorado.)

(I CAN'T GET NO) SATISFACTION

Use Suggested Strum Pattern #4
ot Fingerlpicking Pattern #6

Words and Music by
MICK JAGGER and KEITH RICHARDS

Moderately

142

(I Can't Get No) Satisfaction - 4 - 3

Verse 2:
When I'm watchin' my TV,
And a man comes on and tells me
How white my shirts can be,
But he can't be a man 'cause he doesn't smoke
The same cigarettes as me.
I can't get no, oh, no, no, no.
Hey, hey, hey, that's what I say.
(To Chorus:)

Verse 3:
When I'm ridin' 'round the world,
And I'm doin' this and I'm signin' that,
And I'm tryin' to make some girl
Who tells me, baby, better come back maybe next week,
'Cause you see I'm on a losin' streak.
I can't get no, oh, no, no, no.
Hey, hey, hey, that's what I say.
I can't get no...
(To Outro:)

(I Can't Get No) Satisfaction - 4 - 4

SHE LOVES YOU

Use Suggested Strum Pattern #2

Moderately bright

Words and Music by
JOHN LENNON and PAUL McCARTNEY

Verse 2:
She said you hurt her so she almost lost her mind.
But now she says she knows you're not the hurting kind.
She said she loves you and you know that can't be bad.
Yes, she loves you and you know you should be glad, oo.
(To Chorus:)

Verse 3:
You know it's up to you, I think it's only fair.
Pride can hurt you too, apologize to her.
Because she loves you and you know that can't be bad.
Yes, she loves you and you know you should be glad, oo.
(To Chorus:)

SHOWER THE PEOPLE

Use Suggested Strum Pattern #6
or Fingerpicking Pattern #6

Words and Music by
JAMES TAYLOR

Moderately

Shower the People - 3 - 1

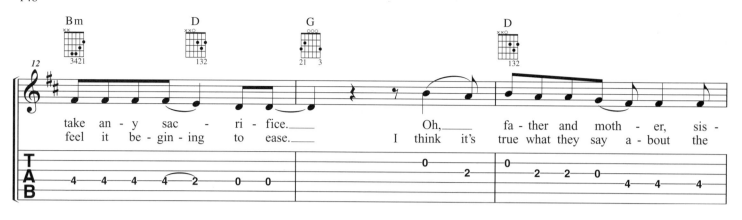

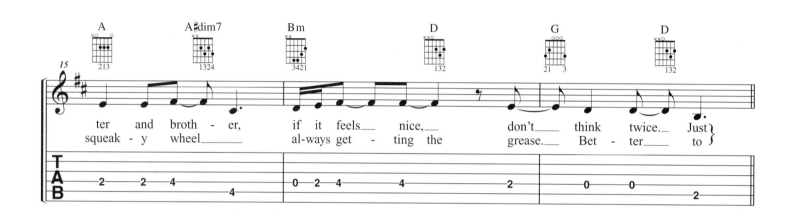

Chorus:

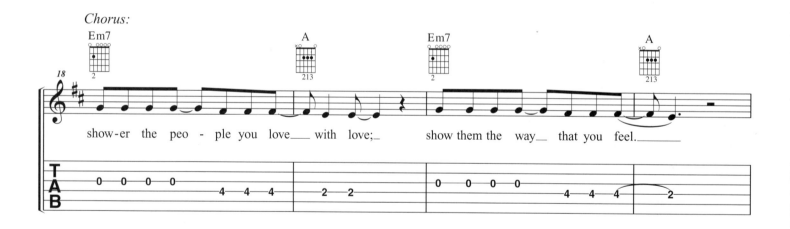

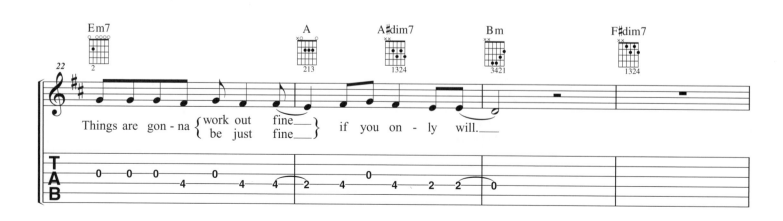

SPACE ODDITY

**Use Suggested Strum Pattern #6
or Continue Intro Pattern Simile**

Words and Music by
DAVID BOWIE

Moderately slow

Play 4 times

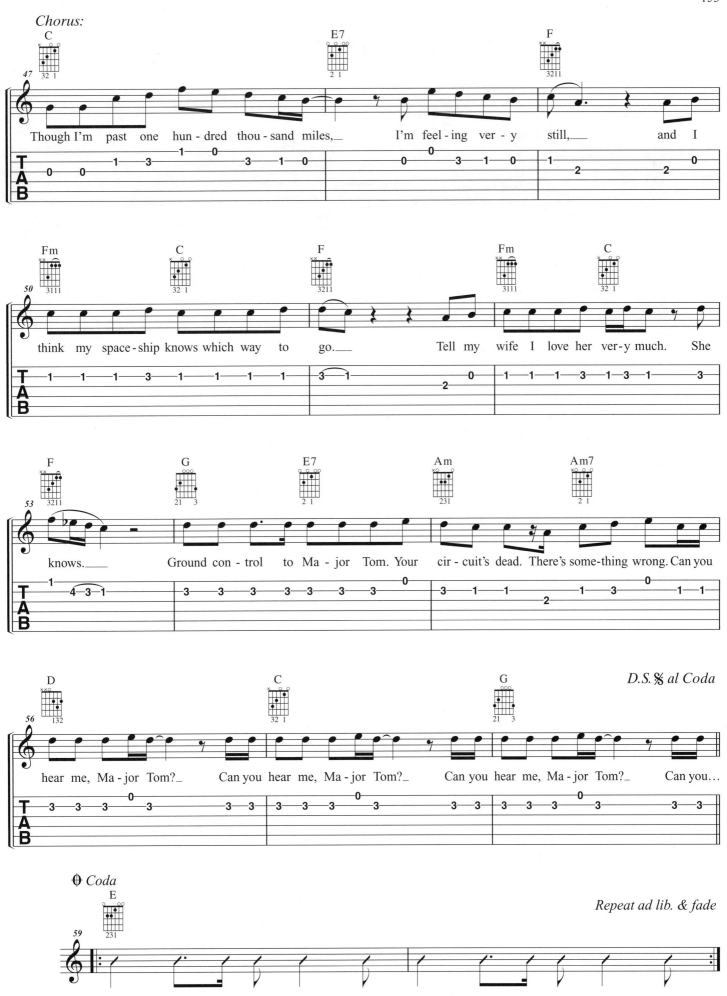

STAIRWAY TO HEAVEN

(Excerpt)

Use Suggested Strum Pattern #3

Words and Music by
JIMMY PAGE and ROBERT PLANT

Slowly

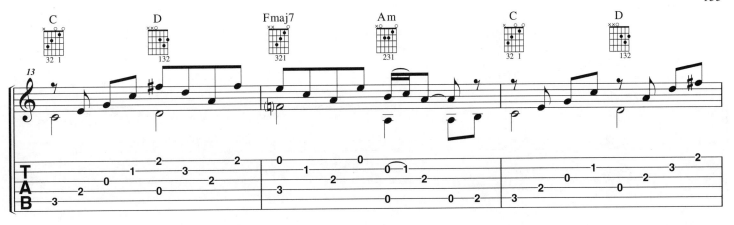

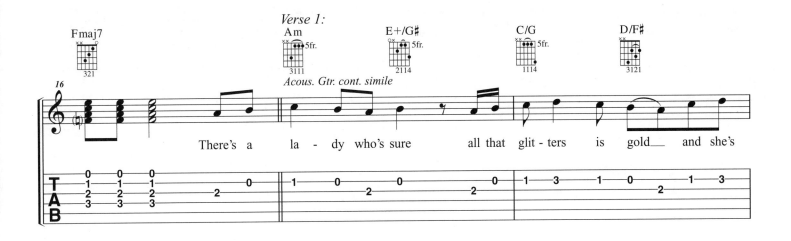

Verse 1:

There's a la - dy who's sure all that glit - ters is gold___ and she's

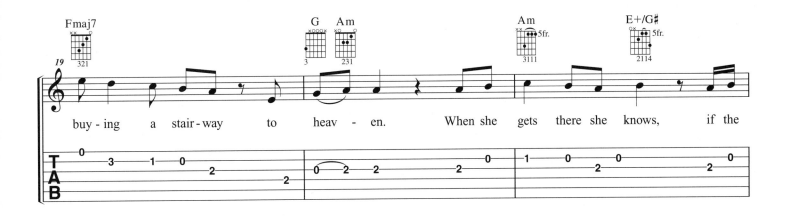

buy - ing a stair - way to heav - en. When she gets there she knows, if the

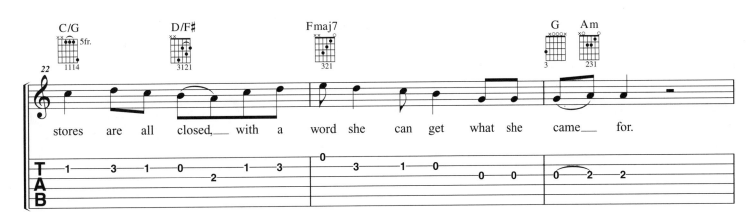

stores are all closed,___ with a word she can get what she came___ for.

STAND BY YOUR MAN

Use Suggested Strum Pattern #4

Words and Music by
TAMMY WYNETTE and BILLY SHERRILL

Moderate country swing

SUPERSTAR

Words and Music by
LEON RUSSELL, BONNIE BRAMLETT
and DELANEY BRAMLETT

TAKE ME HOME, COUNTRY ROADS

Use Suggested Strum Pattern #3
Moderately bright

Verse:

Words and Music by
JOHN DENVER, BILL DANOFF
and TAFFY NIVERT

Take Me Home, Country Roads - 3 - 1

TIME OF THE SEASON

Use Suggested Strum Pattern #4

Moderately

Words and Music by
ROD ARGENT

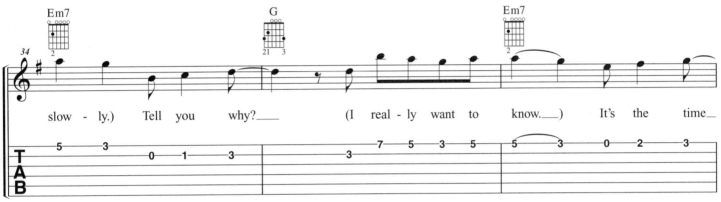

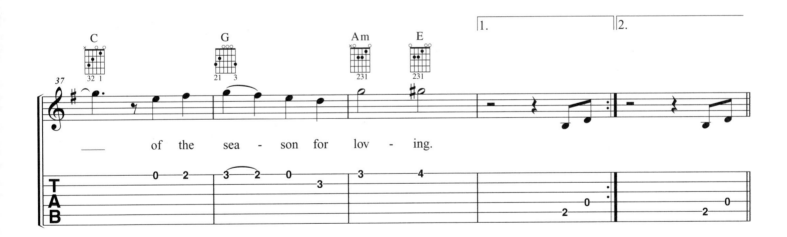

Outro:
Organ Solo:

Repeat ad lib. & fade

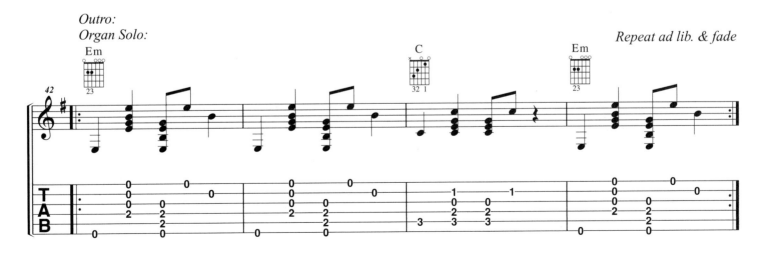

A WHITER SHADE OF PALE

Words and Music by
KEITH REID and GARY BROOKER

Use Suggested Strum Pattern #5

Moderately slow

A Whiter Shade of Pale - 3 - 1

Verse 2:
She said, "There is no reason
And the truth is plain to see."
But I wandered through my playing cards,
And would not let her be
One of sixteen vestal virgins
Who were leaving for the coast.
And, although my eyes were open,
They might have just as well've been closed.
And so it was that later,
As the miller told his tale,
That her face, at first just ghostly,
Turned a whiter shade of pale.

A Whiter Shade of Pale - 3 - 3

WILD HORSES

Use Suggested Strum Pattern #3
or Continue Intro Pattern Simile

Words and Music by
MICK JAGGER and KEITH RICHARDS

Moderately slow

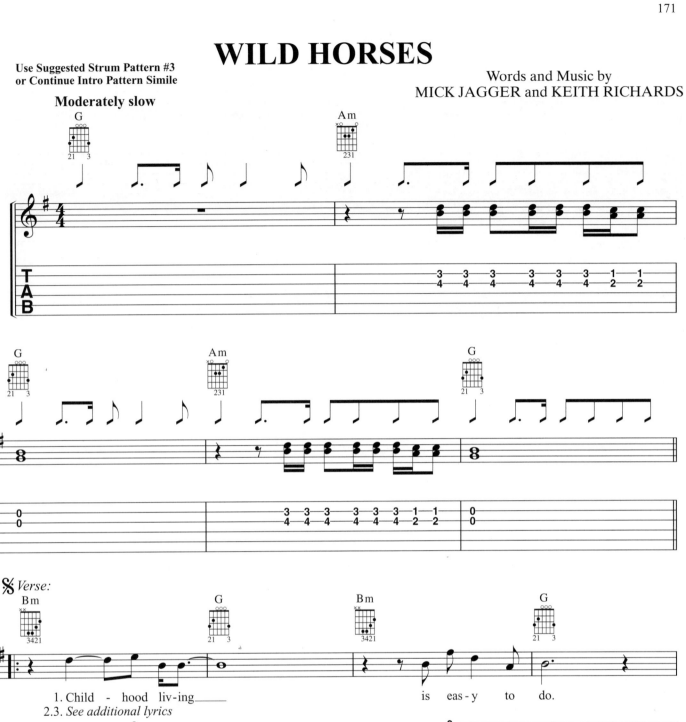

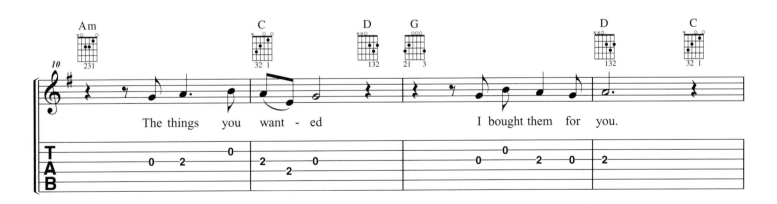

Wild Horses - 3 - 1

Verse 2:
I watched you suffer a dull aching pain.
Now you decided to show me the same.
No sweeping exits or offstage lines
Could make me feel bitter, or treat you unkind.
(To Chorus:)

Verse 3:
I know I dreamed you a sin and a lie.
I have my freedom, but I don't have much time.
Faith has been broken, tears must be cried.
Let's do some living after we die.
(To Chorus:)

WIPE OUT

Use Suggested Strum Pattern #1
Moderately

By THE SURFARIS

Wipe Out - 2 - 1

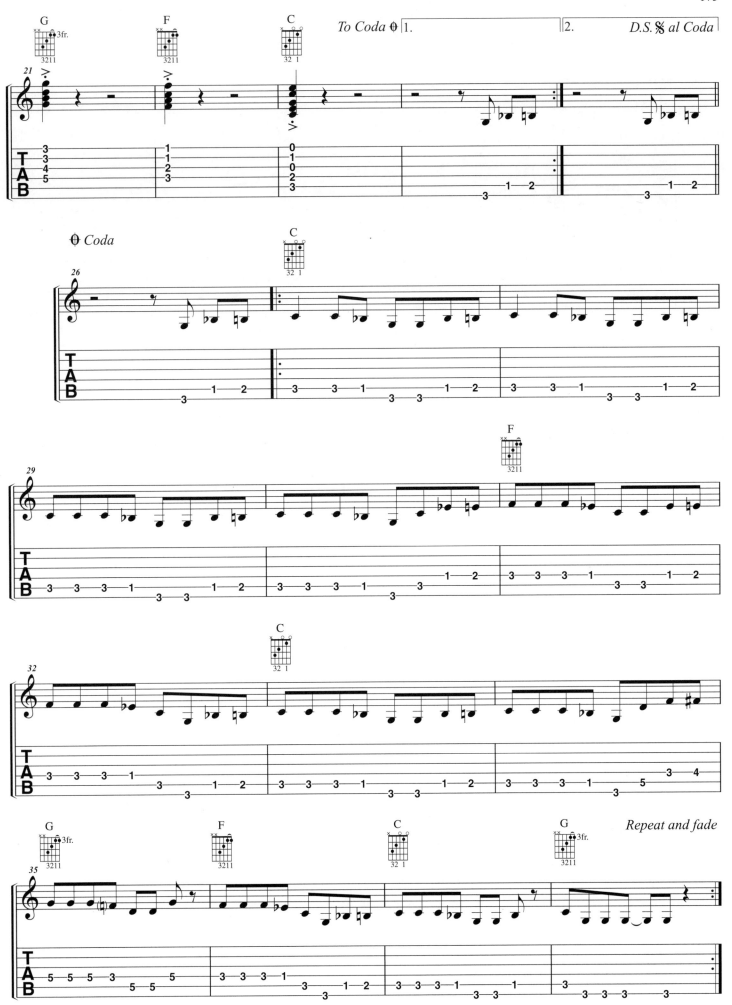

WOODSTOCK

**Use Suggested Strum Pattern #6
or Fingerpicking Pattern #6**

Words and Music by
JONI MITCHELL

Moderately

1. Well, I came__ __ up-on__ a child__ of God,__ he was walk-ing a-long__ the road__ and__ I asked__

2.3. *See additional lyrics*

__ him, "Tell me where are you go - ing?" this he told__ me: said, "I'm go -

- ing down__ to Yas - gur's Farm,__ gon-na join__ in a rock and roll__ band.__ Got to

Verse 2:
Well, then can I walk beside you? I have come to lose the smog.
And I feel as if a cog in something turning.
And maybe it's the time of year, yes, and maybe it's the time of man.
And I don't know who I am but life is for learning.
(To Chorus:)

Verse 3:
By the time we got to Woodstock, we were half a million strong,
And everywhere was a song and a celebration.
And I dreamed I saw the bomber jet planes riding shotgun in the sky,
Turning into butterflies above our nation.
(To Chorus:)

WITH ARMS WIDE OPEN

**Use Suggested Strum Pattern #1
or Fingerpicking Pattern from Intro**

Words and Music by
MARK TREMONTI and SCOTT STAPP

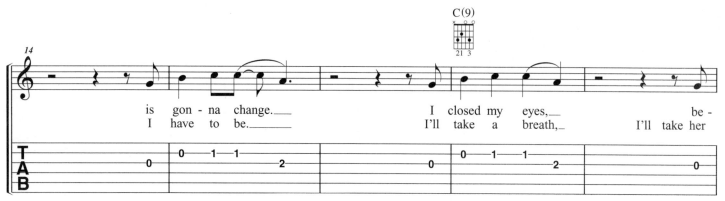

With Arms Wide Open - 5 - 1

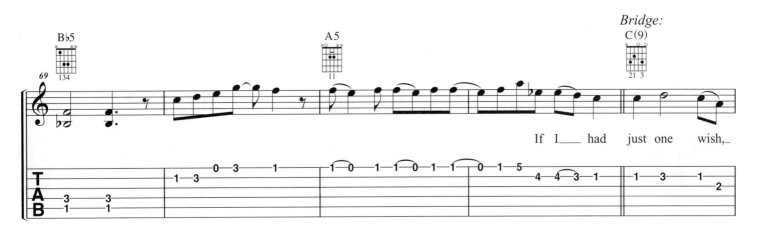

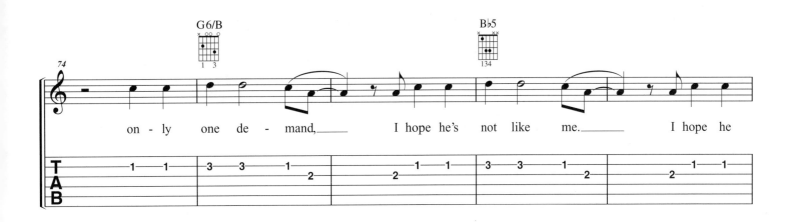

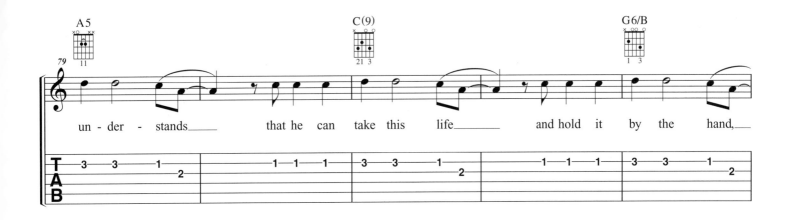

GUITAR TAB GLOSSARY

TABLATURE EXPLANATION

TAB illustrates the six strings of the guitar.
Notes and chords are indicated by the placement of fret numbers on each string.

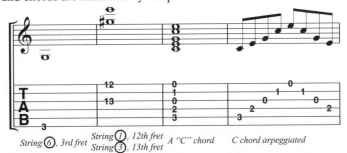

String ⑥, 3rd fret   String ①, 12th fret   A "C" chord   C chord arpeggiated
String ③, 13th fret

BENDING NOTES

Half Step:
Play the note and bend string one half step (one fret).

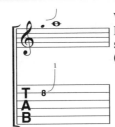

Whole Step:
Play the note and bend string one whole step (two frets).

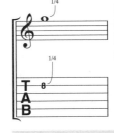

Slight Bend/ Quarter-Tone Bend:
Play the note and bend string sharp.

Prebend and Release:
Play the already-bent string, then immediately drop it down to the fretted note.

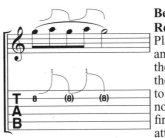

Bend and Release:
Play the note and bend to the next pitch, then release to the original note. Only the first note is attacked.

PICK DIRECTION

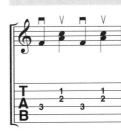

Downstrokes and Upstrokes:
The downstroke is indicated with this symbol (⊓) and the upstroke is indicated with this (∨).

ARTICULATIONS

Hammer On:
Play the lower note, then "hammer" your finger to the higher note. Only the first note is plucked.

Pull Off:
Play the higher note with your first finger already in position on the lower note. Pull your finger off the first note with a strong downward motion that plucks the string—sounding the lower note.

Palm Mute:
The notes are muted (muffled) by placing the palm of the pick hand lightly on the strings, just in front of the bridge.

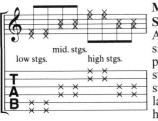

Muted Strings:
A percussive sound is produced by striking the strings while laying the fret hand across them.

Legato Slide:
Play the first note and, keeping pressure applied on the string, slide up to the second note. The diagonal line shows that it is a slide and not a hammer-on or a pull-off.

HARMONICS

Natural Harmonic:
A finger of the fret hand lightly touches the string at the note indicated in the TAB and is plucked by the pick producing a bell-like sound called a harmonic.

RHYTHM SLASHES

Strum Marks/ Rhythm Slashes:
Strum with the indicated rhythm pattern. Strum marks can be located above the staff or within the staff.

Single Notes with Rhythm Slashes:
Sometimes single notes are incorporated into a strum pattern. The circled number below is the string and the fret number is above.

Artificial Harmonic:
Fret the note at the first TAB number, lightly touch the string at the fret indicated in parens (usually 12 frets higher than the fretted note), then pluck the string with an available finger or your pick.